Time for

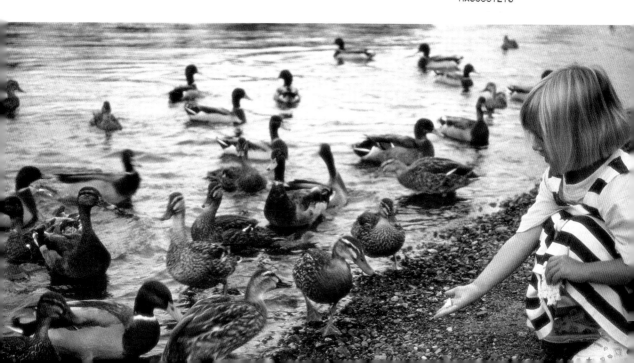

Meow, meow.

Here we come!

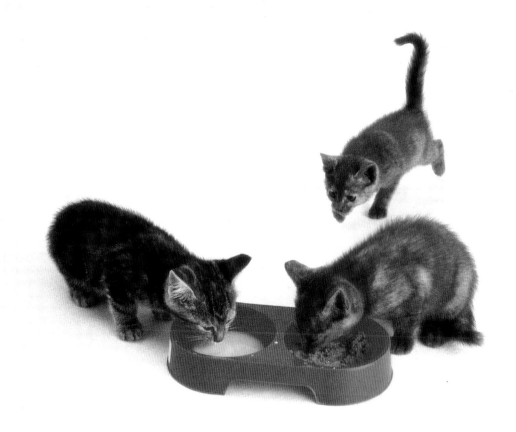

Woof, woof.

Here we come!

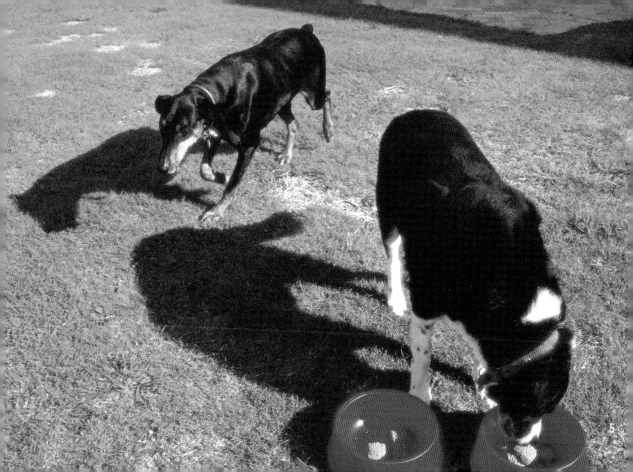

Baa, baa.

Here we come!

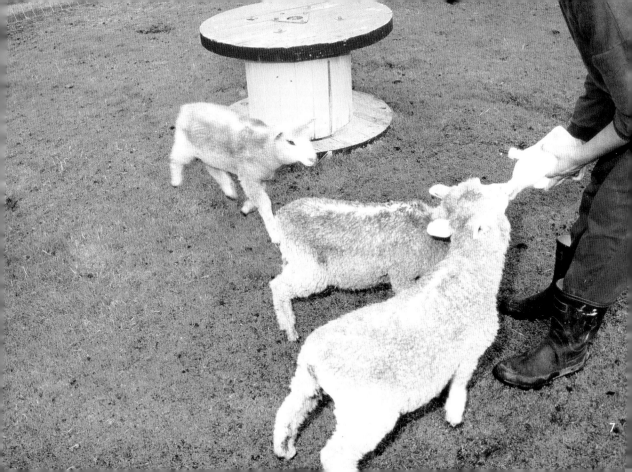

Oink, oink.

Here we come!

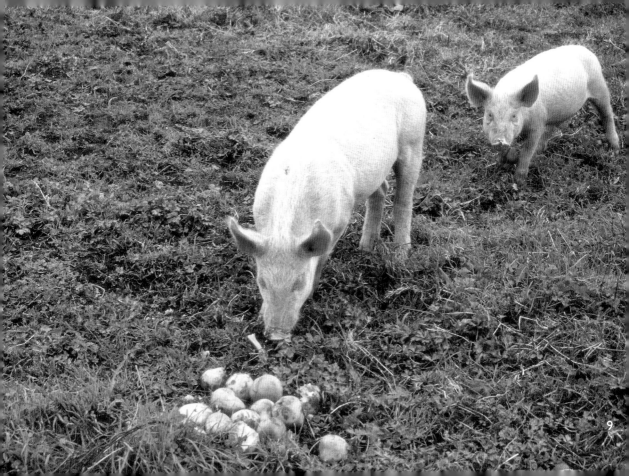

Moo, moo.

Here we come!

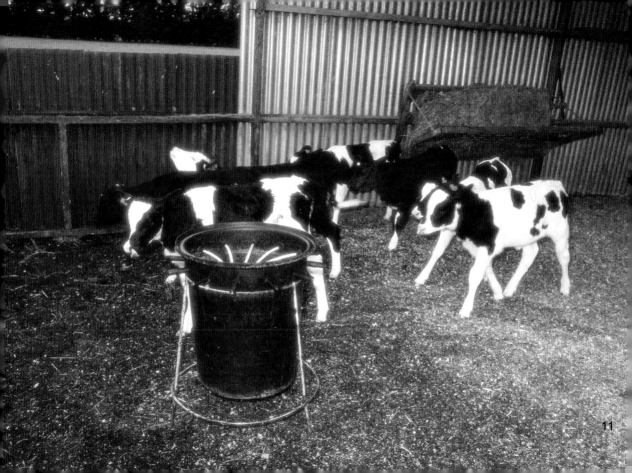

Quack, quack.

Here we come!

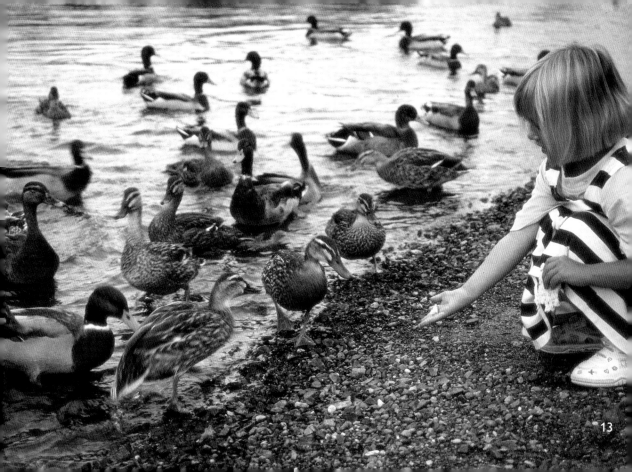

Cluck, cluck.

Here we come!

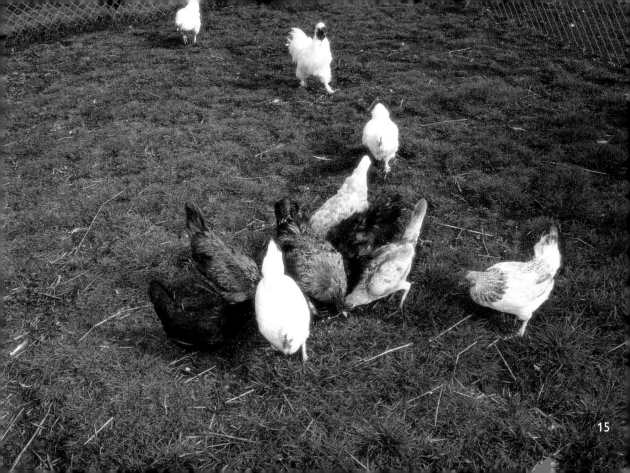

15

Here we come!

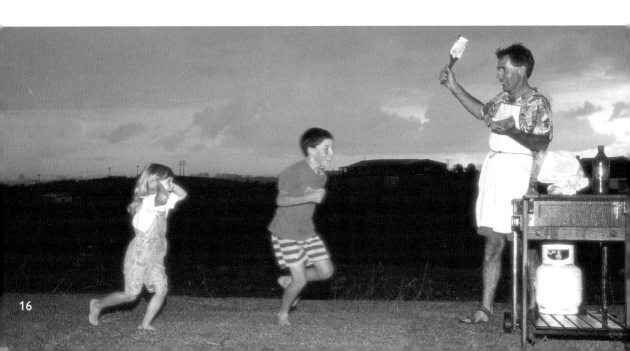